THE OFFICIAL
CRYSTAL PALACE
ANNUAL 2019

To Eli,
Happy 6th
birthday!
Lots of love
from Cinde
+ Auntie
Fiona
× ×

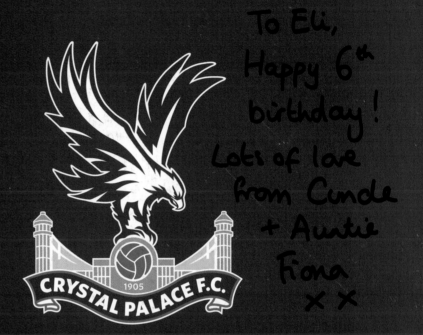

Written by James Bandy

A Grange Publication

© 2018. Published by Grange Communications Ltd., Edinburgh, under licence from Crystal Palace Football Club. Printed in the EU.

Special thanks to Ian King and Peter Hurn.

Photographs © Crystal Palace FC, Reuters, Press Association & Shutterstock.

ISBN: 978-1-912595-05-1

CONTENTS

PALACE STARS ON INSTAGRAM!

WITH PATRICK VAN AANHOLT

PALACE'S DUTCH STAR RATES AND SLATES HIS TEAM-MATES' INSTAGRAM PAGES!

@JEFFREYSHCLUPP

PVA SAYS:
"Jeff's Instagram is actually alright! I like this – I'll give you this. I'm not sure about that picture. I like this one where he's engaging with his son. It's all about family. It's important. And he spends time with his boys as well. I like his style, it's alright!"

PVA SAYS:
"He doesn't post a lot, does he? He's got like 17 pictures! Dead! Scott Dann – no!"

@SCOTTDANN06

@JRIEDEWALD

PVA SAYS:
"Man's got no posts! He's got 43k followers but no posts. That's good going! Jairo's my boy, though. He's got good style and you can have a laugh with him."

6

© Wayne Hennessey Instagram

@WAYNEHENNESSEY

PVA SAYS:

"It says on his post that he's happy to sign a new deal, but he doesn't look very happy! Look at his face! You think this is happy when you've signed a new deal? This is a nice picture, though. He could have let it go, though – the ball was going out! Style, not sure! Recently he's been alright, but he's not up there, to be fair!"

PVA SAYS:

"He doesn't post football pictures, you know! Oh, he does! But he posts mostly about his family and that's a good thing. He's got 1 million followers too. And he's one of the flashiest dressers in the squad. He's up there. His gear sometimes is good, you know. I like his style sometimes."

© Mamadou Sakho Instagram

@MAMADOUSAKHO

© Wilfried Zaha Instagram

@WILFRIEDZAHA

PVA SAYS:

"I like this one – little man Wilf! 'Just a boy with a dream,' it says. I like that. We all had it. I'm not sure about this one, though. No, Wilf's good. He's posting a lot. He's up there! He loves a selfie but he never smiles for the camera!"

GOALS OF THE SEASON!

THERE WERE SOME SUPERB GOALS SCORED BY THE EAGLES IN THE 2017–18 CAMPAIGN – CHECK OUT OUR FAVOURITES HERE!

BAKARY SAKO

V LEICESTER (A)
DECEMBER 16, 2017

With Palace 2-0 up and the game well into time added on, Ruben Loftus-Cheek was sent clear down the left. He got to the edge of the penalty area and squared the ball to Bakary, who curled the ball into the top corner via the post.

LUKA MILIVOJEVIC

V SOUTHAMPTON (A)
JANUARY 2, 2018

Palace were drawing 1-1 with Southampton going into the last ten minutes. After good work down the right, the ball was squared to Luka 25 yards out, and the Serbian almost passed the ball into the net with a curling shot that left the keeper rooted to the spot.

BAKARY SAKO

V BRIGHTON (A)
JANUARY 8, 2018

In an FA Cup tie third round against our big rivals, Sako brought ball down on the left hand side midway in Brighton's half. He looked up, and without even taking a touch hit an unstoppable drive that flew past the keeper and in off the far post.

PATRICK VAN AANHOLT

V MAN. UNITED (H)
MARCH 5, 2018

The Eagles were already 1-0 up against United when they were awarded a free-kick just inside The Red Devils' half. Quick-thinking Jeff Schlupp set PVA free down the left, and the full-back showed ice-cool finishing to beat De Gea at his near post.

LUKA MILIVOJEVIC

V BOURNEMOUTH (A)
APRIL 7, 2018

When Palace won a free-kick centrally about 25 yards from goal, top scorer Milivojevic stepped up to take it. With just a two-step run-up, he curled a glorious free-kick up and over the wall and into the corner of the net.

WILFRIED ZAHA

V BOURNEMOUTH (A)
APRIL 7, 2018

Picking the ball up inside Bournemouth's penalty area, Wilf dribbled his way past two players out of the 18-yard box, pulled off an audacious Around The World to beat a third before hitting a curling left-foot strike into the top corner!

WILFRIED ZAHA

V BRIGHTON (H)
APRIL 14, 2018

Milivojevic picked up a clearance halfway inside the Brighton half and curled a lovely cross into the penalty area. Sensing the opportunity, Zaha got between two Brighton defenders at the far post to score with an awesome diving header!

WILFRIED ZAHA

V LEICESTER (H)
APRIL 28, 2018

A brilliant passing move that started down Palace's left-hand side reached the edge of Leicester's penalty area. Cabaye rolled the ball back under his foot and Zaha was there to open his body up and hit a right-foot shot into the roof of the net!

WORDFIT

CAN YOU FIT THESE AWESOME 20 PALACE STRIKERS INTO THE GRID?

ARMSTRONG

BENTEKE

BRIGHT

BYRNE

CHERRETT

CLARKE

DAWES

FORSSELL

FREEDMAN

GAYLE

JOHNSON

KUQI

MORRISON

MURRAY

PHILLIPS

SHIPPERLEY

SIMPSON

SMITH

SWINDLEHURST

WRIGHT

CHECK THE SOLUTION ON PAGE 60

SPOT THE DIFFERENCE
CAN YOU SPOT THE NINE DIFFERENCES BETWEEN THESE TWO PICTURES?

CHECK THE SOLUTION ON PAGE 60

SEASON REVIEW 2017-18

THE 2017-18 SEASON WAS ANOTHER ROLLERCOASTER FOR PALACE FANS. THERE ARE ALWAYS PLENTY OF UPS AND DOWNS, BUT AT LEAST IT'S NEVER BORING!

AUGUST

Hopes were high when Frank de Boer was named Palace's new manager in the summer of 2017. The Dutchman, who had won three league titles in four years in charge of Ajax, was seen as the type of young, progressive coach that would take Palace to the next level. Summer signings Mamadou Sakho, Jairo Riedewald, and the arrival of Ruben Loftus-Cheek and Timothy Fosu-Mensah on loan also pointed towards a new style of play under the new manager. But the optimism was short-lived. A 3-0 opening day home defeat to new boys Huddersfield was followed by a 1-0 defeat to Liverpool and a 2-0 reverse at Swansea in the Premier League, meaning the Eagles finished the month at the foot of the Premier League with no points and no goals. Indeed, their only success came in the Carabao Cup as they beat Ipswich 2-1, with James McArthur scoring both goals.

SEPTEMBER

After five games and 77 days, the club parted ways with Frank de Boer following a 1-0 defeat at Burnley. In his place Croydon-born Roy Hodgson, who started his career at Palace, took over as manager. But if fans thought a change of manager would see an immediate change in fortunes, they would be disappointed. A 1-0 defeat at home to Southampton was followed by a 5-0 loss away at Manchester City, before they travelled to Manchester the following week to take on United, only to lose 4-0. Once again, the only ray of light came in the Carabao Cup, where a Bakary Sako goal was enough to see off Huddersfield and put The Eagles into the next round. Performances had improved, but there were still no points to show for it, and the tally of no Premier League goals was a big worry.

OCTOBER

A trip to Champions Chelsea wouldn't seem the likeliest place to pick up a first win of the season, but that's exactly what happened. Azpilicueta's own goal was cancelled out by Bakayoko's shot seven minutes later, but Wilfried Zaha's strike on the stroke of half-time sealed their first Premier League points of the season. A 1-0 defeat to Newcastle followed, before Palace suffered a 4-1 Carabao Cup defeat at Bristol City, but they ended the month more positively, coming back from 2-0 down at home to West Ham to claim a point thanks to Zaha's last-minute goal.

NOVEMBER

November was a month of slow progress for The Eagles. It started with a 1-0 defeat at the hands of Tottenham, but the work-rate, discipline and togetherness was encouraging. A 2-2 draw at home to Everton followed, where McArthur and Zaha twice gave Palace the lead only to be pegged back each time. A second win of the season, and the first at home, came when Stoke visited Selhurst Park, with The Eagles coming back from 1-0 down to snatch an injury-time winner with thanks to Mamadou Sakho's close-range strike. The month ended with a trip to rivals Brighton, their first meeting in the Premier League, but despite the hype before the game, it ended in a 0-0 draw. But after the lows of the first few months of the season, November was definitely a positive.

SEASON REVIEW 2017-18

DECEMBER

December was a busy month, and a very good one at that, even if it did start with a drab 0-0 draw against West Brom, managed by former boss Alan Pardew. The following Saturday saw The Eagles draw 2-2 at home to Bournemouth, with three goals coming in four crazy first-half minutes just before half-time. But the real story came at the end, when Christian Benteke's last-minute penalty was saved by The Cherries' keeper. If that was a disappointment, it was all forgotten the following week. On the Tuesday, The Eagles came from 1-0 down to beat Watford 2-1 and on the Saturday, Palace's first Premier League away goal of the season arrived at Leicester. It was scored by Benteke, which was also the Belgian's first strike of the campaign. If that wasn't sweet enough, a dominant performance saw The Eagles win 3-0 thanks to further goals from Zaha and Sako. A draw at Swansea and a 3-2 defeat at home to Arsenal followed, before The Eagles hosted champions-elect Manchester City on New Year's Eve. Despite only having 25 per cent possession, Palace put in a superb performance to earn a 0-0 draw and end City's 18-game winning run, and it could have been even better if Ederson hadn't saved Milivojevic's injury-time penalty. Even so, the month suggested better times were around the corner.

JANUARY

The new year certainly started that way, with a 2-1 win at Southampton. An FA Cup trip to Brighton followed, but in a hard-fought game, former Eagle Glenn Murray scored the late goal which put Palace out of the cup. Back in the Premier League, things continued to look up. A 1-0 home win over Burnley, thanks to Bakary Sako's strike, took Palace up to 12th after just one defeat in the previous 12 games. But if anyone was getting too excited, The Eagles got a reality check the following week on their visit to The Emirates to take on Arsenal. The Gunners raced into a 4-0 half-time lead and despite a better second half display and a goal from Milivojevic, Palace lost 4-1. A trip to the London Stadium and a 1-1 draw with West Ham saw Roy Hodgson's side finish the month in 12th position, but more worryingly, only three points above the relegation zone.

FEBRUARY

February wasn't a great month for The Eagles. It started with a 1-1 draw at home to Newcastle, where Palace needed a second-half Milivojevic penalty to claim a point, followed by a 3-1 defeat away to Everton, with Luka on the scoresheet again with another penalty. The month ended with Tottenham coming to Selhurst. In a game where Palace only had 24 per cent of the possession, they held Spurs until two minutes from time when Harry Kane's header gave the visitors a 1-0 win. The result left Palace in 17th position, level on points with 18th-placed Stoke.

MARCH

With The Eagles hovering just above the relegation zone, March looked a tough month. They hosted Manchester United and Liverpool, as well as facing champions Chelsea at Stamford Bridge, with only a visit to Huddersfield giving respite. And so it proved. The Eagles lost to Manchester United in heart-breaking fashion, going 2-0 up only to lose 3-2 thanks to a Nemanja Matic strike in the last minute. A 2-1 defeat to Chelsea followed, before Palace beat Huddersfield 2-0 away from home thanks to goals from James Tomkins and Luka Milivojevic. The result was huge – it hauled The Eagles out of the relegation zone, to within one point of Huddersfield and within six points of 10th. A win at home to Liverpool at the end of the month would have been the icing on the cake but, despite taking a 13th minute lead through a Milivojevic penalty, The Reds came back to win 2-1, with Mane and Salah scoring second half goals. The result left Palace two points above the relegation zone with six games left.

APRIL

April began with a trip to the South Coast to take on Bournemouth, but despite taking the lead twice, first through Milivojevic and then Zaha, Palace had to settle for a point after a last-minute Josh King strike saw the game end 2-2. The following weekend saw the visit of Brighton, and what a game it was. The Eagles stormed into a 2-0 lead after 14 minutes thanks to goals from Zaha and Tomkins, only for Murray to pull a goal back four minutes later. Zaha's strike after 24 minutes restored the two-goal lead, only for Izquierdo to make it 3-2 – and all this in the first half. The second half was goalless, meaning Palace claimed all three points and jumped to 16th in the table. A 0-0 draw at Watford followed, before possibly the performance of the season. Leicester arrived at Palace in poor form, but the response from The Eagles was ruthless. Zaha's 17th minute opener was doubled by McArthur after 38 minutes, before three goals in the last ten minutes from Loftus-Cheek, Van Aanholt and Benteke sealed a memorable win. The victory took The Eagles to 11th with two games remaining, and though a few teams below could technically still catch them, it certainly eased a lot of worries around Selhurst Park.

MAY

Palace confirmed their place in next season's Premier League and ended Stoke's ten-year stay in the division with a 2-1 win at the Britannia Stadium. Xherdan Shaqiri opened the scoring with a free-kick, but second-half goals from James McArthur and Patrick van Aanholt meant Palace stayed up at the expense of their hosts. This relieved the pressure ahead of the last game of the season, a home fixture against relegated West Brom, who had been demoted the previous week. Second-half goals from Zaha and Van Aanholt secured a 2-0 win and an 11th-placed finish, which looked incredibly unlikely only a few months earlier.

PALACE LEGENDS
NO.1

JIM CANNON

DATE OF BIRTH: 02.10.53
PLACE OF BIRTH: GLASGOW, SCOTLAND
POSITION: CENTRE-BACK
PLAYED: 1973-1988
SIGNED FROM: TRAINEE
GAMES: 660
GOALS: 36

The term legend is often used too easily, but in this case it couldn't be more true. For 15 years, Jim Cannon seemed to be a near ever-present in the heart of Palace's defence.

After coming through the ranks at Palace, he made a goalscoring debut on March 31, 1973 against Chelsea. Cannon went on to make 660 appearances for the club, breaking Terry Long's record of 480 during the 1984-85 season, and went on to make nearly 200 more. He was captain for his last ten seasons at the club and epitomised everything that was good about Palace.

As a defender he was tall and imposing, but his presence suggested he was even bigger than he was. On the pitch he made everything look so easy, and had that ability to be in the right place at the right time to snuff out danger. While he only scored 36 goals in his 15 seasons at the club, they always seemed to be crucial goals in crucial games.

In 2005 Cannon was voted into the club's Centenary XI, and was only just pipped to 'The Player of the Century' award by Ian Wright. Jim Cannon – a proper Palace legend.

WILFRIED ZAHA

1. IN WHICH YEAR DID WILF MAKE HIS PALACE DEBUT –
   2010, 2011 OR 2012?

2. WHICH MASSIVE CLUB DID THE WICKED WIDE MAN JOIN IN 2013?

3. WHAT SHIRT NUMBER DOES WILF WEAR FOR PALACE?

4. ZAHA HAS TWO INTERNATIONAL CAPS FOR ENGLAND. TRUE OR FALSE?

5. WHICH TEAM DID HE SCORE HIS FIRST GOAL OF THE 2017-18 SEASON
   AGAINST?

CHECK THE ANSWERS ON PAGE 60

A NEW PALACE TO CALL HOME!

AN AMAZING NEW CHAPTER IN THE HISTORY OF CRYSTAL PALACE IS ABOUT TO BEGIN WITH THE REDEVELOPMENT OF SELHURST PARK!

Work on the new main stand is due to begin at the end of the 2018-19 season and be finished by the summer of 2021 so The Eagles can begin the 2021-22 season in their awesome, updated home!

The project will increase the capacity at Selhurst Park from 26,000 to more than 34,000, overhauling a stadium which has been the club's home since 1924. It will transform the match-day experience for supporters and provide new facilities for the community while retaining the ground's uniquely passionate Premier League atmosphere.

The centrepiece of the redevelopment is a stunning new five-storey stand featuring an all-glass front – paying homage to the club's earliest days when it stood in the shadows of the original Crystal Palace, erected on Sydenham Hill. A central vaulted arch, with the famous Eagle crest, is a reminder of the iconic 1851 Exhibition Hall, and eagle wings flank the 41-metre structure.

Check out some pictures and all the facts and stats you need to know about the redevelopment!

PITCH PERFECT

A bigger pitch, increased from 101.5m x 68, to 105m x 68m, making Selhurst Park compliant with UEFA regulations and eligible to host tournament football.

THE TUNNEL CLUB

Premium hospitality and entertainment facilities for more than 2,500 supporters, including a new Tunnel Club, and between 16-28 boxes, which will give members a unique vantage point as the players prepare for the match and conduct post-match interviews.

£75 MILLION

The project is estimated to cost between £75 million and £100 million.

FOR THE COMMUNITY

New community facilities, supplementing the work of the Palace for Life Foundation, which delivers health, education and sporting programmes for more than 13,500 local children and young adults.

13,500

Capacity in the new stand will increase from around 5,400 to 13,500, with more than 10,700 General Admission seats – an increase of around 6,000.

34,000

The overall capacity of the stadium will be increased from 26,000 to 34,000.

WORTH THE WAIT

Improved sightlines in the Arthur Wait Stand with the removal of the TV gantry, and improved Arthur Wait concourse.

CRYSTAL PALACE STARS...
SNAPPED!
THESE PALACE STARS LOVE BEING IN FRONT OF THE CAMERA!

THE BOSS DOES HIS BEST ED SHEERAN IMPRESSION FOR THE CROWD!

CHRISTIAN BENTEKE NEEDS TO GO TO SPECSAVERS!!

"NAH RY, WE DON'T NEED TO KNOW WHICH WAY THE CHAMPIONSHIP IS."

PVA LOOKS PRETTY HAPPY TO HAVE BEATEN HIS FORTNITE RECORD SCORE...

WILF TRIES TO HAIL A TAXI AFTER BEING CHOPPED DOWN ONE TIME TOO MANY...

"VARDY AIN'T HAVING NO PARTY TONIGHT, MAMA."

MAMA'S SO IN CONTROL HE CAN SHOW WATFORD A BIT OF BREAKDANCING...

"I WANT YOU TO DROP AND GIVE ME 100 SIT-UPS, BOY!"

DON'T EVEN THINK ABOUT MESSING WITH KARATE KID WILF...

ROY CAN'T BELIEVE HE FORGOT TO SKY+ EASTENDERS...

THE LATE-NIGHT OKEY COKEY WENT DOWN A STORM WITH THE PLAYERS...

AND PVA'S NOT TOO HAPPY ABOUT IT, EITHER!

WHEN YOUR MASCOT PUTS THE GLOVES ON AT HALF-TIME, HE'S A KEEPER...

THE REFEREE DROPPED AN EGGY ONE AND THERE WERE INSTANT CASUALTIES...

ROY PERFECTS HIS DEATH STARE ON FORMER PALACE BOSS SAM ALLARDYCE...

SNAPPED!

"SO YOU TAKE THE SECOND LEFT, THIRD EXIT AT THE ROUNDABOUT AND IT'S ON THE RIGHT. YOU CAN'T MISS IT."

"NOW YOU SEE IT, NOW YOU DON'T." WIZARD WILF PUTS ANOTHER ONE ON THE DECK.

"I KNOW YOU'D LOVE TO JOIN ME AT PALACE, CHRIS, BUT IT'S NOT HAPPENING."

PALACE ANAGRAMS!

REARRANGE THE LETTERS TO REVEAL THESE EAGLES HEROES!

1. TCOST ANND

2. STARCHINI BEEKNET

3. MUMDAAO KASHO

4. FREEFYJ PCPLUSH

5. RONCON HACKIMW

6. KULA VOICEJIMLIV

7. AIRJO AWILDDEER

8. JONAS NUNECHOP

9. SEMAJ CRAMHURT

10. WILDFIRE HAAZ

CHECK THE SOLUTION ON PAGE 60

FACE IN THE CROWD!

CAN YOU SPOT THESE PALACE PLAYERS MINGLING IN THE HOLMESDALE?

- ☐ ANDROS TOWNSEND
- ☐ LUKA MILIVOJEVIC
- ☐ SCOTT DANN
- ☐ MAMADOU SAKHO
- ☐ CHRISTIAN BENTEKE
- ☐ JAMES MCARTHUR

- ☐ PATRICK VAN AANHOLT
- ☐ WILFRIED ZAHA

CHECK THE SOLUTION ON PAGE 61

CRYSTAL PALACE'S...
BEST EVER STRIKERS!

PALACE HAVE BEEN LUCKY ENOUGH TO HAVE SOME GREAT FRONT MEN OVER THE YEARS, BUT WHO'S THE BEST? CHECK OUT OUR TOP PICKS!

DOUGIE FREEDMAN

1995–1997 & 2000–2008
GOALS: 108   GAMES: 368
GAMES PER GOAL: 3.41

The Scot's goals helped Palace clinch promotion to the top flight in 1997, which included a brilliant double as a late substitute in the play-off win over Wolverhampton Wanderers. Ironically, he joined Wolves a couple of months into Palace's Premier League season but he returned home in 2000 and scored on further memorable occasions, etching himself into Palace folklore with 108 club goals.

CHRIS ARMSTRONG

1992-1995

GOALS: 58   GAMES: 136

GAMES PER GOAL: 2.34

Armstrong was a speedy forward who was an instant success in his first campaign at Selhurst Park, grabbing 15 goals in 36 matches during Palace's first Premier League season in 1992-93. Unfortunately it wasn't enough, and The Eagles were relegated. But he fired Palace back up the following season, with The Eagles winning the league, and then netted 15 times the following season in the Premier League, though Palace were relegated again. He was eventually sold to Tottenham Hotspur for a then record-breaking fee of £4.5million.

CLINTON MORRISON

1997-2002 & 2005-2008

GOALS: 113   GAMES: 316

GAMES PER GOAL: 2.80

Morrison marked his professional debut in style by coming off the bench as a teenager at home to Sheffield Wednesday and notching a last-minute winner. Palace had already been relegated at that point, but fans were to see more of the confident striker's goals in two spells at the club, netting 113 times for The Eagles.

DAVE SWINDLEHURST

1973-1980

GOALS: 81   GAMES: 276

GAMES PER GOAL: 3.41

Swindlehurst came up through the ranks at Palace, making his debut as a raw 17-year-old before developing into a fearsome striker who was key in Palace's promotion to the First Division for the first time in 1979. Big, strong, superb in the air but capable of scoring great goals with his feet, too, the striker was the club's top scorer or joint-top scorer for four consecutive seasons from 1976 to 1979. Palace through and through, Swindlehurst will forever be a Palace hero.

CRYSTAL PALACE'S...
BEST EVER STRIKERS! CONTINUED

JOHNNY BYRNE

1956-1962 & 1967-1968
GOALS: 101   GAMES: 259
GAMES PER GOAL: 2.56

Byrne started his career at Palace and spent six seasons at the club, establishing himself as a firm fans' favourite. He finished top scorer in the 1959-60 season with 19 goals, and then again in the 1960-61 campaign as the club were promoted from Division Four. The striker left for West Ham in 1962 having scored 96 goals for the club, then a post-war record, before returning for the 1967-68 season.

PERCY CHERRETT

1925-1927
GOALS: 65   GAMES: 81
GAMES PER GOAL: 1.25

Cherrett joined the club from Plymouth in 1925 and was Palace's top scorer for the next two seasons. He hit 33 goals in his first season – a club record at the time – as Palace finished mid-table in Division Three South, and followed it up with 32 goals the following season. He also scored two hat-tricks while at the club, and has the second best goals-per-game ratio of any Palace player in history, behind Peter Simpson.

TED SMITH

1911-1920

GOALS: 124   GAMES: 192

GAMES PER GOAL: 1.55

Smith, a Birmingham-born striker Palace signed from Hull, is rightly considered one of the club's best ever strikers. He joined the club when they were in the Southern League, but hit nine goals in Palace's Third Division South Championship winning season of 1921-22.

ANDY JOHNSON

2002-2006 & 2014-2015

GOALS: 85   GAMES: 161

GAMES PER GOAL: 1.89

AJ scored an amazing 21 times during the 2004-05 Premier League, which is still a record for a Palace player in the Premier League. His total also saw him finish the season as the top-scoring English player in the league, but it wasn't enough as Palace were relegated on the final weekend at Charlton. Opposing defenders couldn't cope with his pace and he was brought down for a number of penalties, which he converted himself.

ALBERT DAWES

1933-1936 & 1938-1939

GOALS: 92   GAMES: 156

GAMES PER GOAL: 1.70

Originally signed as a replacement for the injured Peter Simpson, Albert Dawes soon went about making his own mark at Crystal Palace. In his first spell at the club the striker scored 75 goals in just 105 games. His best season was in 1935-36 when he was Division Three South's top scorer with 38 strikes, a feat that earned him a call-up to the England squad. Dawes left for Luton that year before returning in 1938 for one more season and although he couldn't repeat the feats of his first spell at the club, his legacy at the club was assured.

CRYSTAL PALACE'S...
BEST EVER STRIKERS! CONTINUED

PETER SIMPSON

1929-1935

GOALS: 165   GAMES: 195

GAMES PER GOAL: 1.18

Palace's all-time record goalscorer, Simpson first came to Palace's attention when he played against them for Kettering in the first round of the FA Cup in 1928. Despite not scoring, he impressed manager Fred Mavin enough to secure his services, and the rest is history. He scored a hat-trick on his debut against Norwich, and then went on to break all kinds of Palace scoring records, including scoring six goals in a game, 19 hat-tricks in all and being top scorer for five seasons on the trot, as well as the all-time record goalscorer.

MARK BRIGHT

1986-1992

GOALS: 113   GAMES: 286

GAMES PER GOAL: 2.53

It's hard to believe that Steve Coppell signed the striker for just £50,000 from Leicester in 1986. He was the Second Division's top scorer in 1988, and helped the club to promotion the following season. The striker formed a lethal partnership with Ian Wright and went on to score 113 goals over six years with the club, including Palace's first ever Premier League goal in a 3-3 draw at home to Blackburn, before moving to Sheffield Wednesday in 1992.

PALACE'S #1 STRIKER!

IAN WRIGHT

1985–1991

GOALS: 117   GAMES: 277

GAMES PER GOAL: 2.37

Wright was at Selhurst Park for six seasons, and in that time ensured his legend status. After signing from non-league Greenwich Borough three months short of his 22nd birthday in 1985, he went on to score a total of 117 goals in 277 appearances, including an 18-minute hat-trick against Wimbledon. His pace, determination, work-rate and quality finishing meant he also went on to win England caps, reach an FA Cup final and become Palace's record post-war goalscorer.

PALACE LEGENDS
NO.2

JOHNNY BYRNE

DATE OF BIRTH: 13.05.39
PLACE OF BIRTH: WEST HORSLEY, SURREY, ENGLAND
POSITION: STRIKER
PLAYED: 1956-62 & 1967-68
SIGNED FROM: TRAINEE
GAMES: 259
GOALS: 101

Johnny Byrne was another player who came through the ranks to become a huge player for Palace. Born in 1939, he made his debut in 1956 and went on to play 14 times that season, scoring once in Division Three South.

Over the next few seasons he established himself as a key player and huge fans' favourite. In the 1958-59 season, when Palace was a founder member of the new Division Four, Byrne hit 17 goals in 45 matches.

Despite not being particularly big or physical, Byrne was able to ride challenges with balance and agility, and possessed a natural ability on the ball few people had seen at Palace at the time.

In the 1960-61 season the striker hit 30 of Palace's 110 goals as they gained promotion to the Third Division. While at the club Byrne was called up to the England team and made his debut in a 1-1 draw with Northern Ireland, despite playing his football outside the top two divisions.

It was clear that the striker was destined for bigger things, and it was no surprise when West Ham smashed the Second Division transfer record to sign him for £65,000 in 1962. He left the club having scored 96 goals, which was then a post-war record.

He returned in 1967, and in two seasons scored the goals to take him to 101 for the club before moving to Fulham.

MAMADOU SAKHO

1. IN WHICH YEAR WAS SAKHO BORN –
   1988, 1990 OR 1992?

2. WITH WHICH FRENCH CLUB DID HE START HIS FOOTBALL CAREER?

3. WHICH COUNTRY DOES THE TOUGH DEFENDER PLAY FOR?

4. SAKHO SCORED ONE PREMIER LEAGUE GOAL IN 2017-18—
   WHO WAS IT AGAINST?

CHECK THE ANSWERS ON PAGE 61

MEET THE SUMMER SIGNINGS!

THE EAGLES SIGNED FOUR TOP PLAYERS IN THE SUMMER TRANSFER WINDOW, AND HERE WE GIVE YOU THE LOWDOWN ON ALL OF THEM!

JORDAN AYEW

BORN: 11 SEPTEMBER 1991
COUNTRY: GHANA
SIGNED FROM: SWANSEA
FEE: LOAN
SQUAD NO.: 14
HEIGHT: 182CM
WEIGHT: 80KG
BOOTS: NIKE MERCURIAL SUPERFLY VI

Jordan started his career at Marseille, where he marked his senior debut against Lorient in 2009 with a goal in a 2-1 win. The club won the Ligue 1 title at the end of that season, and just 10 months after his first appearance, Jordan won his first Ghana cap.

In 2014-15, his displays caught the attention of Aston Villa, who were looking for a new striker following Christian Benteke's departure to Liverpool. The Villans signed him for £8 million, and he hit seven Premier League goals in his first season before switching to Swansea City in January 2017.

Ayew hit 11 goals for The Swans last term to finish top scorer, which included goals home and away against Palace, and won the Players' Player of the Year award.

STATS

74 PACE

74 SHOOTING

70 PASSING

78 DRIBBLING

31 DEFENDING

74 PHYSICALITY

MAX MEYER

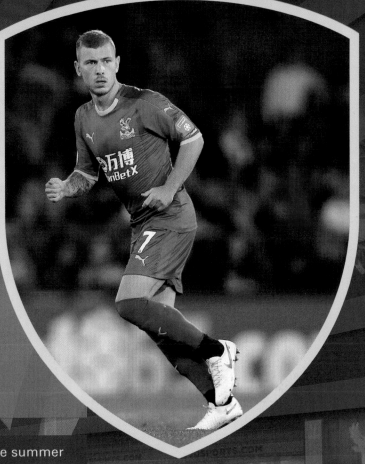

BORN: 18 SEPTEMBER 1995
COUNTRY: GERMANY
SIGNED FROM: FREE AGENT
FEE: FREE
SQUAD NO.: 7
HEIGHT: 173CM
WEIGHT: 60KG
BOOTS: NIKE MAGISTA OPUS

Palace snapped up Meyer in the summer of 2018 after his Schalke 04 contract came to an end.

Capped four times by his country, he made 192 appearances for the German side, including three UEFA Champions League campaigns. During that time he netted 22 goals and provided 24 assists, helping them to finish runners-up in last season's Bundesliga.

At international level, the midfielder was the top scorer and Player of the Tournament as Germany finished runners-up at the European Under-17 Championship in 2012, and then won the Under-21 Euros in 2017, where he was named in the Team Of The Tournament.

Meyer made the step up to the full national side in 2014 and has gone on to win four caps.

STATS

72 PACE
62 SHOOTING
77 PASSING
84 DRIBBLING
35 DEFENDING
53 PHYSICALITY

MEET THE SUMMER SIGNINGS!

CONTINUED...

CHEIKHOU KOUYATE

BORN: 21 DECEMBER 1989
COUNTRY: SENEGAL
SIGNED FROM: WEST HAM
FEE: £9.5 MILLION
SQUAD NO.: 8
HEIGHT: 192CM
WEIGHT: 75KG
BOOTS: NIKE TIEMPO LEGEND VII

The Senegal international captain switched from east to south London in August 2018 after he left West Ham United for Palace.

Kouyate was no stranger to Eagles fans, having represented the Hammers 129 times in the Premier League across four seasons, scoring 12 goals, including the first ever at the London Stadium.

The central midfielder represented FC Brussels, Kortrijk and Anderlecht earlier in his career, winning four league titles in five seasons with the latter. He has also won 42 caps for Senegal since making his debut in 2012, playing in the 2012 Olympics, two Africa Cup of Nations and the 2018 World Cup, where he played in all three of his side's group games.

STATS

83 PACE

66 SHOOTING

68 PASSING

70 DRIBBLING

80 DEFENDING

90 PHYSICALITY

VICENTE GUAITA

BORN: 10 JANUARY 1987
COUNTRY: SPAIN
SIGNED FROM: GETAFE
FEE: FREE
SQUAD NO.: 31
HEIGHT: 190CM
WEIGHT: 80KG
BOOTS: ADIDAS PREDATOR 18.1

Palace made the Spanish shot-stopper their first signing of the summer of 2018 after he penned a three-year deal.

Guaita started his career at Valencia, where he made his first-team bow in 2008-09. He eventually established himself as first-choice, and after helping them to successive third-place finishes in La Liga, he was made vice-captain for the 2013-14 campaign.

At the end of that season he moved to Getafe, where he was instantly installed as their No.1.

After relegation in 2015-16 Guaita helped them bounce back via the play-offs in 2017, and then established them back amongst Spanish football's elite last term by keeping 12 clean sheets to help Getafe to an eighth-place finish.

STATS

72 DIVING
74 HANDLING
73 KICKING
75 REFLEXES
51 SPEED
71 POSITIONING

PALACE'S PRE-SEASON!

THE PALACE SNAPPER FOLLOWED THE LADS THROUGHOUT THEIR PRE-SEASON CAMPAIGN. CHECK OUT THE PICTURES!

Palace's stars warm-up before training starts in Sweden.

The boss keeps a keen eye on proceedings.

The lads warm up in their pre-season training camp.

Roy makes his point clear during a training drill.

Andros fires in a shot during the session.

Julian Speroni gets put through his paces in goal.

Wilfried Zaha keeps his eye on the ball during training.

Pape Souare gets ready to whip a ball into the box.

Wilf takes on anyone who dares try to tackle him!

Benteke watches the ball all the way on to his chest.

PALACE'S PRE-SEASON!

Jeff Schlupp makes a splash in the friendly with FC Helsingor.

The boss has a headache to sort in the friendly against Oxford.

The boss gives the fans a wave at the FC Helsingor friendly.

Wickham's back! Connor looking focused as he arrives at the Madejski Stadium.

Being Palace boss is thirsty work!

Yoohoo! Palace legend Mark Bright in the crowd against Stevenage.

Johnny Williams inspects the pitch – and the matchday programme – before the Reading game.

What's Andros Townsend finding so funny during the game against Reading?

Palace fans soak up the sun watching the boys at The Kassam Stadium.

The boss is looking slick as he turns up for the Reading friendly.

WORDSEARCH

CAN YOU FIND THESE PALACE STARS FROM THE 2018-19 SEASON IN THE GRID BELOW?

```
R C I V E J O V I L I M M R
A S R W S O U A R E W P H R
K N S M A X W K J I U P N E
A I P C T R F C C N J N T Y
S K E A Q W D K C P A T O E
S M R R Y K H H P D E L W M
I O O T R A E U M M K O N K
B T N H M O L L N Y E H S G
N Z I U N H O V L G T N E F
A H Y R C C J H W Y N A N T
W V C S W C L J K J E A D R
H E N N E S S E Y A B N M G
W M K Z Y W D Z B X S A H H
T Y D L A W E D E I R V M P
```

AYEW	MCARTHUR	SAKHO	TOWNSEND
BENTEKE	MEYER	SCHLUPP	VAN AANHOLT
DANN	MILIVOJEVIC	SOUARE	WAN-BISSAKA
HENNESSEY	PUNCHEON	SPERONI	WARD
KELLY	RIEDEWALD	TOMKINS	WICKHAM

CHECK THE SOLUTION ON PAGE 61

GUESS WHO

CAN YOU TELL WHO THESE PALACE PLAYERS ARE?

1.

2.

3.

4.

5.

6.

7.

8.

9.

CHECK THE ANSWERS ON PAGE 61

PALACE WONDERKIDS!

THERE ARE SOME GREAT YOUNG TALENTS COMING THROUGH THE EAGLES' DEVELOPMENT AND ACADEMY SQUADS RIGHT NOW. CHECK OUT THE PLAYERS WHO COULD BE THE STARS OF THE FUTURE!

NYA KIRBY

POSITION: MIDFIELD
COUNTRY: ENGLAND
BORN: 31.01.2000
SIGNED: 18.07.17

2017-18 STATS:
U23S - 18 APPEARANCES, 4 GOALS
U18S - 2 APPEARANCES, 1 GOAL

Kirby was a member of England's victorious U17 World Cup-winning squad in 2017, and the midfielder played in six of their seven games in India, scoring the crucial penalty in a shootout win against Japan in the last-16.

The midfielder signed a professional deal with The Eagles in February 2017, having previously been on the books of Tottenham Hotspur, and quickly earned himself a professional deal after impressing for the development side.

He was named on the first-team bench against his former club Spurs in February 2018, but despite featuring for Roy Hodgson's team in friendly action during the summer of 2018, he is still awaiting his professional debut.

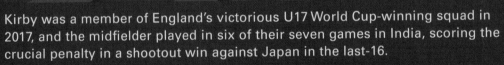

JOSEPH HUNGBO

POSITION: MIDFIELD
COUNTRY: ENGLAND
BORN: 15.01.2000
SIGNED: 24.04.2009

2017-18 STATS:
U23S - 8 APPEARANCES, 1 GOAL
U18S - 29 APPEARANCES, 17 GOALS

As captain of the under-18 side, Hungbo top-scored for his side with 17 goals to fire Palace to the U18 Professional Development League South title in 2017-18.

The winner of the club's Under-16 Player Of The Year award in 2015-16, the direct left-winger came through the Oasis Shirley Park programme and has an eye for goal, helped by his explosive pace.

His performances last season saw him follow up on a couple of initial development team appearances gained during 2016-17, and now he has his chance to make the step up after signing his first professional deal in the summer of 2018.

JAMES DALY

POSITION: FORWARD
COUNTRY: ENGLAND
BORN: 12.01.2000
SIGNED: 29.05.14

2017-18 STATS:
U23S - 13 APPEARANCES, 9 GOALS
U18S - 18 APPEARANCES, 5 GOALS

The striker enjoyed a meteoric rise during 2017-18, as he stepped up from the under-18s to fire the development side to the league title, and be named on the first-team bench for the trip to Bournemouth in April 2018.

Daly has been at The Eagles since under-14 level and is a left-footed player who is comfortable on the wing or centre-forward.

Having scored goals for the under-18s as a 16-year-old, he continued to find the net in subsequent seasons but really found his feet when called up by Richard Shaw for the second half of the 2017-18 campaign, and bagged a hat-trick against Queens Park Rangers to prove he has the quality to step up.

That fine form saw him handed the club's Scholar Of The Year award at the end of a campaign that saw him claim league winner's medals at both under-18 and under-23 levels, and handed a one-year professional deal.

PALACE WONDERKIDS!

CONTINUED...

WILL DONKIN

POSITION: MIDFIELD
COUNTRY: CHINESE TAIPEI
BORN: 26.12.2000
SIGNED: 11.03.17

2017-18 STATS:
U-18S – 10 APPEARANCES

Signed from Chelsea at the end of the 2016-17 season, the midfielder is good on the ball, especially in tight areas. He also boasts a good range of passing and will be looking to try and get plenty of action as he gets to grips with under-18s football.

During his first season with The Eagles, Donkin was capped at full international level for Chinese Taipei against Turkmenistan in November 2017 and has continued to be named in their subsequent squads.

NIKOLA TAVARES

POSITION: DEFENDER
COUNTRY: CROATIA
BORN: 17.01.1999
SIGNED: 08.02.17

2017-18 STATS:
U23S – 9 APPEARANCES

Despite an injury-hit 2017-18 campaign, Tavares' resilience and displays in red and blue saw him handed a contract extension during the summer of 2018.

A Croatian under-18 international, the centre-back was handed a first professional contract with The Eagles after impressing for the under-18s and later the development team on trial in 2016.

He was previously on the books of Hellenic FC before moving to England with Brentford, but was forced to search for a new club once their academy closed in the summer of 2016.

LUKE DREHER

POSITION: MIDFIELDER
COUNTRY: ENGLAND
BORN: 27.11.1998
SIGNED: 21.06.07

2017-18 STATS:
U23S - 2 APPEARANCES

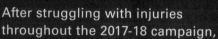

After struggling with injuries throughout the 2017-18 campaign, Dreher will be hoping he can put those setbacks behind him as he aims to get his promising start to life in SE25 back on track.

The central midfielder enjoyed a fine 2015-16 as he came through the academy side to become a regular in the development team despite being only 17, and was named on the first-team bench for the Premier League game at Man. United in April 2016.

The following month he won the club's Under-18 Player Of The Year, and played for the first-team in pre-season. He was once again named on the bench for The Eagles' trip to Middlesbrough in September, but then injuries plagued his progression over the following 18 months.

KIAN FLANAGAN

POSITION: MIDFIELDER
COUNTRY: REPUBLIC OF IRELAND
BORN: 29.08.1999
SIGNED: 01.07.16

2017-18 STATS:
U23S - 25 APPEARANCES, 2 GOALS

The tricky midfielder continued his development by stepping up to the Republic of Ireland's under-19 squad during 2017-18, having previously represented them at under-18 level.

Flanagan has been tipped for big things at The Eagles since making his development team debut aged just 15 towards the end of the 2014-15 season.

Since then he has shared his time between the under-18s and the under-23s and was named as Palace's Scholar Of The Year in 2016-17 before establishing himself as a key member of Richard Shaw's under-23 side the following campaign.

CRYSTAL PALACE...
DID YOU KNOW?

CHECK OUT THESE WEIRD AND WONDERFUL FACTS ABOUT THE EAGLES!

When they were formed in 1905, the club played their home games inside the historic Crystal Palace grounds, which was then the venue for the FA Cup final!

The club was a little late to the party when it came to introducing a club crest. Although their initials were embroidered on the team's shirts from 1935, it actually wasn't until 1955 that the first version of the badge appeared, featuring the Crystal Palace façade.

Want to know how Palace can win the Premier League? Play James Tomkins and Mamadou Sakho together! The Eagles rarely lose a game when the two defenders line up together!

The club is the only one out of the 92 Football League clubs not to have a vowel in the first five letters of its name!

Goalscoring legend Peter Simpson scored a hat-trick on his debut for the club back in 1929, and then went on to be the top scorer for each of the next five seasons!

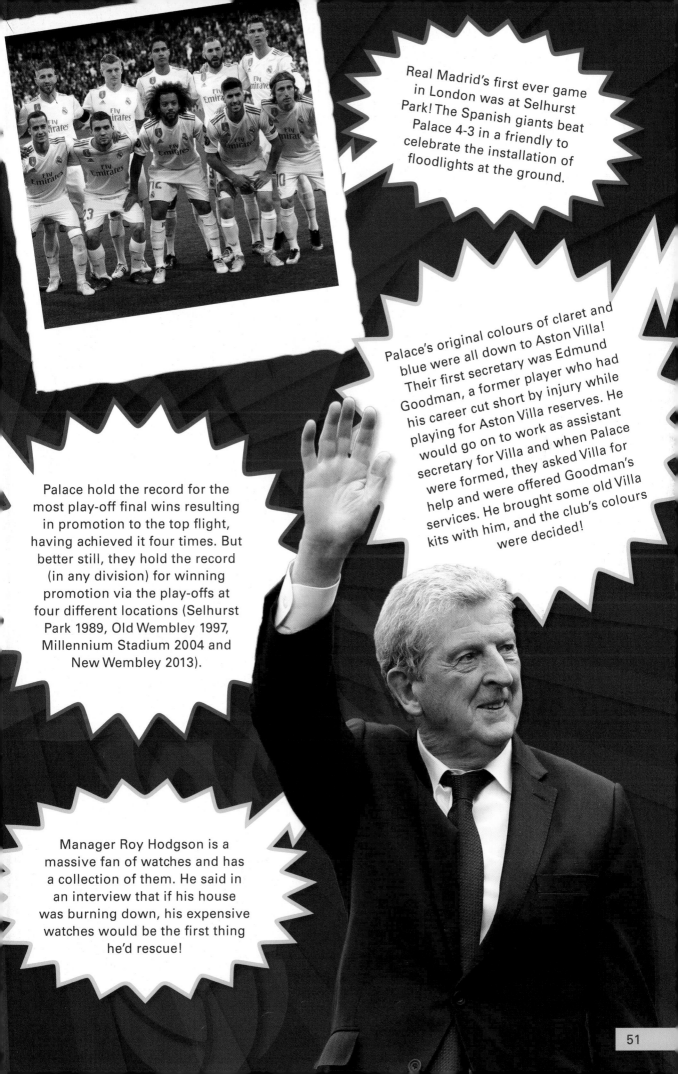

Real Madrid's first ever game in London was at Selhurst Park! The Spanish giants beat Palace 4-3 in a friendly to celebrate the installation of floodlights at the ground.

Palace's original colours of claret and blue were all down to Aston Villa! Their first secretary was Edmund Goodman, a former player who had his career cut short by injury while playing for Aston Villa reserves. He would go on to work as assistant secretary for Villa and when Palace were formed, they asked Villa for help and were offered Goodman's services. He brought some old Villa kits with him, and the club's colours were decided!

Palace hold the record for the most play-off final wins resulting in promotion to the top flight, having achieved it four times. But better still, they hold the record (in any division) for winning promotion via the play-offs at four different locations (Selhurst Park 1989, Old Wembley 1997, Millennium Stadium 2004 and New Wembley 2013).

Manager Roy Hodgson is a massive fan of watches and has a collection of them. He said in an interview that if his house was burning down, his expensive watches would be the first thing he'd rescue!

CRYSTAL PALACE...
DID YOU KNOW?

During the 1959-60 season, Palace earned recognition when goalkeeper Vic Rouse appeared for Wales against Northern Ireland – it made him the first player ever to represent their national team while playing in the fourth division!

Selhurst Park holds the record for the highest attendance for a fourth tier game in English football, when 37,774 people attended the local derby with Millwall in 1961.

The ground also holds the record for the lowest attendance for a Premier League game. However, it wasn't for a Palace game – it was when the club allowed Wimbledon to play there and just 3,039 hardy souls watched them play Everton in 1993.

Star striker Christian Benteke is a massive basketball fan and says his favourite NBA team is the Cleveland Cavaliers because superstar LeBron James used to play for them!

The Eagles are the only club to have been relegated from the Premier League despite finishing fourth from bottom! During the 1994-95 season there were 22 teams in the division, but the Premier League decided to change it to 20 from the 1995-96 season. To balance the Football League they created an extra relegation spot for one season only, and Palace were the unlucky ones!

As if Palace weren't unlucky enough, they also hold the dubious record of being relegated from the Premier League more times than anyone else! They faced the drop in 1993, 1995, 1998 and 2005, and before 2013, had always been relegated the following season after winning promotion.

Palace's red and blue shirts stand out a mile, but they were inspired by Spanish mega club Barcelona! Former boss Malcolm Allison changed the club colours from the original claret and blue to match Barcelona's red and dark blue kit.

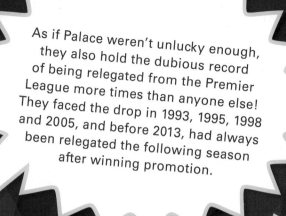

In 1997-98, midfielder Andy Roberts played 37 games in the Premier League and four of them came against Arsenal! He played them twice for Palace, and on another two occasions for Wimbledon.

After the band The Dave Clark Five performed 'Glad All Over' at the stadium in 1968, the fans loved it so much that the song stuck and now it's played before every home game!

Palace wing wizard Andros Townsend started his career at Tottenham, but was released as a 15-year-old. Amazingly, he was recalled just two days later when the old coaches were replaced and the new ones decided they wanted him back!

IAN WRIGHT

DATE OF BIRTH: 03.11.63
PLACE OF BIRTH: WOOLWICH, LONDON, ENGLAND
POSITION: STRIKER
PLAYED: 1985–1991
SIGNED FROM: GREENWICH BORO
GAMES: 277
GOALS: 117

Although Ian Wright was only at Palace for six years, he did more than enough in that time to ensure his legend status at the club.

He signed for The Eagles three months short of his 22nd birthday from Greenwich Borough, but was quick to make up for lost time. After joining the club in 1985, he finished Palace's second highest scorer in his first year.

Blessed with electric pace, acceleration, fantastic movement, a real hunger and an uncanny ability to be in the right place at the right time, the goals kept on flowing.

His partnership up front with Mark Bright was lethal, and largely responsible for Palace getting promotion to the First Division through the play-offs in 1989. During that season Wright scored a total of 33 goals in all competitions, including 24 in the league.

The striker recovered from injury to score twice in the 1990 FA Cup Final against Manchester United after coming on as a substitute. Wright equalised soon after coming on and then put Palace ahead in extra-time, but the game ended 3-3.

During the 1990-91 season Wright gained full England honours, scored his 100th goal for the club and hit an 18-minute hat-trick against Wimbledon as Palace finished third in the First Division, their highest ever finish.

He left for Arsenal in September 1991 for a club record fee of £2.5 million, and by that time was Palace's record post-war goalscorer. In 2005 he was voted into Palace's Centenary XI and was named as their Player of the Century.

ANDROS TOWNSEND

1. WITH WHICH CLUB DID TOWNSEND START HIS FOOTBALL CAREER?

2. WHICH CLUB DID THE SPEEDY WINGER JOIN THE EAGLES FROM?

3. HOW MUCH DID HE COST WHEN HE JOINED
   £13 MILLION OR £10 MILLION?

4. HE TOOK OVER THE NO.10 SHIRT FROM WHICH DEPARTING FANS'
   FAVOURITE?

5. HOW MANY GOALS DID HE SCORE FOR PALACE IN 2017-18?

CHECK THE ANSWERS ON PAGE 61

CRYSTAL PALACE'S...
FIRST-TEAM SQUAD 2018-19

GOALKEEPERS

1. JULIAN SPERONI
Date of birth: 18.05.79
Country: Argentina
Height: 186 cm
Signed: 01.08.04 from Dundee
Fee: £750,000
Palace apps/goals: 403/0

13. WAYNE HENNESSEY
Date of birth: 24.01.87
Country: Wales
Height: 198 cm
Signed: 31.01.14 from Wolves
Fee: £1.6 million
Palace apps/goals: 106/0
Twitter: WayneHennessey1
Instagram: waynehennessey

31. VICENTE GUAITA
Date of birth: 10.01.87
Country: Spain
Height: 190cm
Signed: 01.07.18 (free agent)
Fee: N/A
Palace apps/goals: 0/0

2. JOEL WARD
Date of birth: 29.10.89
Country: England
Height: 188cm
Signed: 29.05.12 from Portsmouth
Fee: £400,000
Palace apps/goals: 205/5
Instagram: joelward2

3. PATRICK VAN AANHOLT
Date of birth: 29.08.90
Country: Holland
Height: 176cm
Signed: 30.01.17 from Sunderland
Fee: Undisclosed
Palace apps/goals: 43/7
Twitter: pvanaanholt
Instagram: patrickvanaanholt

5. JAMES TOMKINS
Date of birth: 29.03.89
Country: England
Height: 192cm
Signed: 05.06.16 from West Ham
Fee: £10 million
Palace apps/goals: 57/6
Instagram: tomkinsofficial

6. SCOTT DANN
Date of birth: 14.02.87
Country: England
Height: 188cm
Signed: 31.01.14 from Blackburn
Fee: £2.5 million
Palace apps/goals: 136/15
Twitter: ScottDann6
Instagram: scottdann06

12. MAMADOU SAKHO
Date of birth: 13.02.90
Country: France
Height: 187cm
Signed: 31.08.17 from Liverpool
Fee: Undisclosed
Palace apps/goals: 28/1
Twitter: mamadousakho
Instagram: mamadousakho

15. JEFFREY SCHLUPP
Date of birth: 23.12.92
Country: Ghana
Height: 178cm
Signed: 13.01.17 from Leicester
Fee: Undisclosed
Palace apps/goals: 43/0
Twitter: Jeffrey_Schlupp
Instagram: jeffreyschlupp

23. PAPE SOUARE
Date of birth: 06.06.90
Country: Senegal
Height: 178cm
Signed: 30.01.15 from Lille
Fee: Undisclosed
Palace apps/goals: 59/0
Twitter: papesouare
Instagram: p.souare_23

29. AARON WAN-BISSAKA
Date of birth: 26.11.97
Country: England
Height: 183cm
Signed: 13.12.16
Fee: From Trainee
Palace apps/goals: 7/0

34. MARTIN KELLY
Date of birth: 27.04.90
Country: England
Height: 191cm
Signed: 14.08.14 from Liverpool
Fee: £2 million
Palace apps/goals: 104/1
Twitter: MartinKelly1990
Instagram: mkelly_34

MIDFIELDERS

7. MAX MEYER
Date of birth: 18.09.95
Country: Germany
Height: 173cm
Signed: Free Agent
Fee: Free Transfer
Palace apps/goals: 0/0
Instagram: maxmeyer95

4. LUKA MILIVOJEVIC
Date of birth: 07.04.91
Country: Serbia
Height: 186cm
Signed: 31.01.17 from
Olympiakos
Fee: Undisclosed
Palace apps/goals: 51/12
Instagram: luka_milivojevic05

8. CHEIKHOU KOUYATE
Date of birth: 21.12.89
Country: Senegal
Height: 189cm
Signed: 01.08.18 from West Ham
Fee: Undisclosed
Palace apps/goals: 0/0
Twitter: PapiCheikhou
Instagram: roilionpapis8

10. ANDROS TOWNSEND
Date of birth: 16.07.91
Country: England
Height: 181cm
Signed: 01.07.16 from Newcastle
Fee: £10 million
Palace apps/goals: 79/5
Twitter: andros_townsend
Instagram: officialtownsend

18. JAMES MCARTHUR
Date of birth: 27.04.90
Country: Scotland
Height: 191cm
Signed: 01.09.14 from Wigan
Athletic
Fee: Undisclosed
Palace apps/goals: 130/16
Twitter: jamesmcarthur16

20. JONATHAN WILLIAMS
Date of birth: 09.10.93
Country: Wales
Height: 168cm
Signed: 01.07.11 from youth
Fee: N/A
Palace apps/goals: 66/1
Instagram: jwills93

44. JAIRO RIEDEWALD
Date of birth: 09.09.96
Country: Holland
Height: 183cm
Signed: 24.07.17 from Ajax
Fee: Undisclosed
Palace apps/goals: 15/0

42. JASON PUNCHEON
Date of birth: 26.06.86
Country: England
Height: 173cm
Signed: 31.01.14 from
Southampton
Fee: £1.75 million
Palace apps/goals: 161/16

25. SULLAY KAIKAI
Date of birth: 27.04.90
Country: England
Height: 191cm
Signed: 14.08.14 from youth
Fee: N/A
Palace apps/goals: 6/1
Twitter: SullayKaikai
Instagram: sullaykakai

CRYSTAL PALACE'S...
FIRST-TEAM SQUAD 2018-19

9. ALEXANDER SORLOTH
Date of birth: 05.12.95
Country: Norway
Height: 193cm
Signed: 31.01.18 from FC Midtjylland
Fee: Undisclosed
Palace apps/goals: 4/0
Twitter: Asorloth
Instagram: asorloth

11. WILFRIED ZAHA
Date of birth: 10.11.92
Country: Ivory Coast
Height: 180cm
Signed: 02.02.15 from Man. United
Fee: Undisclosed
Palace apps/goals: 287/43
Twitter: wilfriedzaha
Instagram: wilfriedzaha

17. CHRISTIAN BENTEKE
Date of birth: 03.12.90
Country: Belgium
Height: 190cm
Signed: 28.08.16 from Liverpool
Fee: Undisclosed
Palace apps/goals: 71/20
Twitter: chrisbenteke
Instagram: christianbenteke

21. CONNOR WICKHAM
Date of birth: 31.03.93
Country: England
Height: 191cm
Signed: 03.08.15 from Sunderland
Fee: Undisclosed
Palace apps/goals: 34/10
Twitter: ConnorWickham10
Instagram: connorwickham21

JORDAN AYEW
Date of birth: 11.09.91
Country: Ghana
Height: 182cm
Signed: 09.08.18 from Swansea City (loan)
Fee: N/A
Palace apps/goals: N/A
Twitter: jordan_ayew9
Instagram: jordanayew9

QUIZ ANSWERS

WORDFIT P.10

cherrett
simpson
kuqi
wright
shipperley
freedman
swindlehurst
morrison
armstrong
murray
dawes
johnson
phillips
benteke
smith
forssell
clarke
bright
gayle
byrne

ANAGRAMS P.26

1. SCOTT DANN
2. CHRISTIAN BENTEKE
3. MAMADOU SAKHO
4. JEFFREY SCHLUPP
5. CONNOR WICKHAM
6. LUKA MILIVOJEVIC
7. JAIRO RIEDEWALD
8. JASON PUNCHEON
9. JAMES MCARTHUR
10. WILFRIED ZAHA

SPOT THE DIFFERENCE P.11

dafabet

WILFRIED ZAHA P.19

1. 2010
2. MAN. UNITED
3. 11
4. TRUE
5. CHELSEA

MAMADOU SAKHO P.35

1. 1990
2. PSG
3. FRANCE
4. STOKE

GUESS WHO P.45

1. CHRISTIAN BENTEKE
2. JAMES MCARTHUR
3. PAPE SOUARE
4. SCOTT DANN
5. LUKA MILIVOJEVIC
6. ANDROS TOWNSEND
7. WAYNE HENNESSEY
8. MAMADOU SAKHO
9. PATRICK VAN AANHOLT

WORDSEARCH P.44

ANDROS TOWNSEND P.55

1. TOTTENHAM
2. NEWCASTLE
3. £10 MILLION
4. YANNICK BOLASIE
5. TWO

WHERE'S KAYLA?

CAN YOU SPOT KAYLA THE EAGLE IN THE CROWD?